ROBERT LAMM SELECTED LYRICS

ROBERT LAMM SELECTED LYRICS

MARMONT LANE
BOOKS

Marmont Lane
BOOKS

ROBERT LAMM SELECTED LYRICS

Copyright © 2020 by Robert Lamm. All rights reserved. No part of this book may be used or reproduced in any matter whatsoever without written permission except in the case of brief quotations embodied in critical articles and reviews.

For information address Marmont Lane Books
139 South Beverly Drive Suite 318
Beverly Hills, CA USA 90212

www.marmontlane.com

FIRST EDITION

Publisher: Bobby Woods/Marmont Lane Books

Design: ♡×♖=⚡

Cover Portrait: Courtesy Robert Lamm Personal Collection

ISBN: 978-0-9998527-7-4

To

JOY LAMM

For inspiring me, challenging me, teaching me, loving me…
and for letting me love her.

ROBERT LAMM SELECTED LYRICS

MARMONT LANE
BOOKS

CONTENTS

INTRODUCTION	13
DOES ANYBODY REALLY KNOW WHAT TIME IT IS?	14
BEGINNINGS	16
QUESTIONS 67 & 68	18
QUESTIONS 67 & 68 (JAPANESE)	20
25 OR 6 TO 4	22
FANCY COLOURS	24
DIALOGUE PT. I + II	26
GOODBYE	28
SATURDAY IN THE PARK	30
SONG FOR RICHARD AND HIS FRIENDS	32
SOMEDAY, I'M GONNA GO	34
HARRY TRUMAN	36
SCRAPBOOK	38
TABLA	40
WILL PEOPLE EVER CHANGE?	42
IF EVERYBODY KNOWS	44
THE LOVE OF MY LIFE	46
SACHA	48
STANDING AT YOUR DOOR	50
SLEEPING IN THE MIDDLE OF THE BED AGAIN	52

SELECTED LYRICS

FEEL THE SPIRIT	54
SAD OLD HOUSE	56
I COULD TELL YOU SECRETS	58
IT'S A GROOVE, THIS LIFE	60
FOR YOU, KATE	62
YOU NEVER KNOW THE STORY	64
ANOTHER TRIPPY DAY	66
COME TO ME, DO	68
I CONFESS	70
HAUTE GIRL	72
HEAVEN IN MY EYES	74
SEAN, IT'S YOUR TURN	76
THE POSSIBILITY OF LIFE	78
SEND RAIN	80
4 BELLS	82
OUT OF THE BLUE	84
ONE DAY ON THE EQUINOX	86
WATCHING ALL THE COLORS IN MY HEAD	88
NAKED IN THE GARDEN OF ALLAH	90
ABOUT THE AUTHOR	93
ACKNOWLEDGEMENTS	95
PUBLISHING	96

ROBERT LAMM

INTRODUCTION

I don't recall how, or why I began writing lyrics. My first songs were perhaps unusual, but sincere. As a primary songwriter for the band Chicago, I experienced overwhelming success during our unexpectedly long sequence of recorded albums.

Music and lyrics are very separate creations. I love doing both. My songs dating from the late '60's through the early 80's provided the opportunity to experiment, learn and develop as a musician. My music evolved, and so did my lyric vocabulary and intentions.

By the late 80's I was urged and encouraged to collaborate with other songwriters, which often yielded good songs but more importantly, yielded lasting friendships. While collaborating on music ideas, I often found myself being the primary lyricist of many songs.

After decades in California, I had found love, and returned to New York City. This was the true start of my life. With inspired energy, I was reaching for honest new territory in a series of solo albums, which contain my best work.

WHY THIS BOOK? I am a man of few spoken words.

While quietly loving them, I wanted our children, Sacha, Kate, and Sean, to know about my journey and my internal life, perhaps best expressed in my lyrics.

In this collection, I purposefully selected songs containing lyrics that are solely of my invention, acknowledging the great collaborations on the music side.

- Santa Monica, California 2019

DOES ANYBODY REALLY KNOW WHAT TIME IT IS?

Chicago, Illinois 1968

SELECTED LYRICS

AS I WAS WALKING DOWN THE STREET ONE DAY
A MAN CAME UP TO ME AND ASKED ME
WHAT THE TIME WAS THAT WAS ON MY WATCH
AND I SAID:

(I DON'T)
DOES ANYBODY REALLY KNOW WHAT TIME IT IS?
(CARE)
DOES ANYBODY REALLY CARE?
(ABOUT TIME)
IF SO, I CAN'T IMAGINE WHY
(OH NO,)
WE'VE ALL GOT TIME ENOUGH TO CRY

AND I WAS WALKING DOWN THE STREET ONE DAY
A PRETTY LADY LOOKED AT ME AND SAID HER
DIAMOND WATCH HAD STOPPED COLD DEAD
AND I SAID:

(I DON'T)
DOES ANYBODY REALLY KNOW WHAT TIME IT IS?
(CARE)
DOES ANYBODY REALLY CARE?
(ABOUT TIME)
IF SO, I CAN'T IMAGINE WHY
(OH NO,)
WE'VE ALL GOT TIME ENOUGH TO CRY

AND I WAS WALKING DOWN THE STREET ONE DAY
BEING PUSHED AND SHOVED BY PEOPLE TRYING TO BEAT THE CLOCK
I JUST DON'T KNOW, I DON'T KNOW, I DON'T KNOW
AND I SAID:

(I DON'T)
DOES ANYBODY REALLY KNOW WHAT TIME IT IS?
(CARE)
DOES ANYBODY REALLY CARE?
(ABOUT TIME)
IF SO I CAN'T IMAGINE WHY
(OH NO,)
WE'VE ALL GOT TIME ENOUGH TO DIE

BEGINNINGS

Hollywood, California 1969

SELECTED LYRICS

WHEN I'M WITH YOU
IT DOESN'T MATTER WHERE WE ARE
OR WHAT WE'RE DOING
I'M WITH YOU THAT'S ALL THAT MATTERS

TIME PASSES MUCH TOO QUICKLY
WHEN WE'RE TOGETHER LAUGHING
I WISH I COULD SING IT TO YOU
I WISH I COULD SING IT TO YOU

MOSTLY, I'M SILENT

WHEN I KISS YOU
I FEEL A THOUSAND DIFFERENT FEELINGS
THE COLOR OF CHILLS
ALL OVER MY BODY

AND WHEN I FEEL THEM
I QUICKLY TRY TO DECIDE WHICH ONE
I SHOULD TRY TO PUT INTO WORDS
OH NO, TRY TO PUT IT INTO WORDS

MOSTLY, I'M SILENT

ONLY THE BEGINNING
OF WHAT I WANT TO FEEL FOREVER
ONLY THE BEGINNING
ONLY JUST THE START

QUESTIONS 67 & 68

Chicago, Illinois 1969

SELECTED LYRICS

CAN THIS FEELING THAT WE HAVE TOGETHER
SUDDENLY EXIST BETWEEN?
DID THIS MEETING OF OUR MINDS TOGETHER
HAPPEN JUST TODAY, SOMEWAY?

I'D LIKE TO KNOW,
CAN YOU TELL ME, PLEASE DON'T TELL ME
IT REALLY DOESN'T MATTER ANYHOW
IT'S JUST THAT THE THOUGHT OF US SO HAPPY
APPEARS IN MY MIND, AS A BEAUTIFULLY MYSTERIOUS THING

WAS YOUR IMAGE IN MY MIND SO DEEPLY
OTHER FACES FADE AWAY?
BLOCKING MEMORIES OF UNHAPPY HOURS
LEAVING JUST A BURNING LOVE

CAN THIS LOVIN' WE HAVE FOUND WITHIN US
SUDDENLY EXIST BETWEEN?
DID WE SOMEHOW TRY TO MAKE IT HAPPEN
WAS IT JUST A NATURAL THING?

I'D LIKE TO KNOW
CAN YOU TELL ME, PLEASE DON'T TELL ME
IT REALLY DOESN'T MATTER ANYHOW
IT'S JUST THAT THE THOUGHT OF US SO HAPPY
APPEARS IN MY MIND, AS A BEAUTIFULLY MYSTERIOUS THING

QUESTIONS 67 AND 68

QUESTIONS 67 & 68

Chicago, Illinois 1969 (Japanese)

SELECTED LYRICS

ふたりの 胸の中で 感じ合うもの
それはとても 不思議な 突然の事
おねがい きかせて その理由(わけ)
だけど どうでも いいさ
この しあわせを 胸に だきしめて
ただ 信じたい 奇蹟を

君の ほほえみだけを きざみつけたい
悲しみは 消えてゆく 心が燃える
おねがい きかせて その理由(わけ)
だけど どうでも いいさ
この しあわせを 胸に だきしめて
ただ 信じたい 奇蹟を

ふたりの 見つけた愛は 突然のもの
それとも これはすべて 理由(わけ)があるのか
おねがい きかせて その理由(わけ)
だけど どうでも いいさ
この しあわせを 胸に だきしめて
ただ 信じたい 奇蹟を

QUESTIONS 67 AND 68

ROBERT LAMM

25 OR 6 TO 4

West Hollywood, California 1970

SELECTED LYRICS

WAITING FOR THE BREAK OF DAY
SEARCHING FOR SOMETHING TO SAY
FLASHING LIGHTS AGAINST THE SKY
GIVING UP, I CLOSE MY EYES
SITTING CROSSLEGGED ON THE FLOOR
TWENTY FIVE OR SIX TO FOUR

STARING BLINDLY INTO SPACE
GETTING UP TO SPLASH MY FACE
WANTING JUST TO STAY AWAKE
WONDERING HOW MUCH I CAN TAKE
SHOULD I TRY TO DO SOME MORE
TWENTY FIVE OR SIX TO FOUR

FEELING LIKE I OUGHT TO SLEEP
SPINNING ROOM IS SINKING DEEP
SEARCHING FO SOMETHING TO SAY
WAITING FOR THE BREAK OF DAY
TWENTY FIVE OR SIX TO FOUR
TWENTY FIVE OR SIX TO FOUR

FANCY COLOURS

Studio City, California 1970

SELECTED LYRICS

GOING WHERE THE ORANGE SUN HAS NEVER DIED
AND YOUR SWIRLING MARBLE EYES SHINE
LAUGHING
BURNING BLUE THE LIGHT
BITTERSWEET THE DROPS OF LIFE
MEMORIES ONLY FADING

FANCY COLOURS
FANCY COLOURS
ARE ALL WE EVER DO SEE
AND WHEN WE'RE DOWN AT THE SEA
WE SEE THINGS SO VERY FINE AT THE SEA

FANCY COLOURS
FANCY COLOURS
ARE ALL WE EVER CAN DO
THE MORNING COVERED WITH DEW
WE DO THINGS SO VERY FINE IN THE DEW

FANCY COLOURS
FANCY COLOURS
ARE ALL WE EVER DO HEAR
BUT WHETHER WE'RE HERE OR THERE
WE HEAR THINGS SO VERY FINE WHEN WE'RE THERE

DIALOGUE PT. I + II

Kansas City, Missouri 1972

SELECTED LYRICS

Q: ARE YOU OPTIMISTIC 'BOUT THE WAY THAT THINGS ARE GOING?
A: NO, I NEVER, EVER THINK OF IT AT ALL

Q: DON'T YOU EVER WORRY WHEN YOU SEE WHAT'S GOING DOWN?
A: NO I TRY TO MIND MY BUSINESS, THAT IS, NO BUSINESS AT ALL

Q: WHEN IT'S TIME TO FUNCTION AS A FEELING HUMAN BEING
WILL YOUR BACHELOR OF ARTS HELP YOU GET BY?
A: I HOPE TO STUDY FURTHER, A FEW MORE YEARS OR SO
I ALSO HOPE TO KEEP A STEADY HIGH

Q: WILL YOU TRY TO CHANGE THINGS, USE THE POWER THAT YOU HAVE
THE POWER OF A MILLION NEW IDEAS?
A: WHAT IS THIS POWER YOU SPEAK OF AND THE NEED FOR THINGS TO CHANGE?
I ALWAYS THOUGHT THAT EVERYTHING WAS FINE

Q: DON'T YOU FEEL REPRESSION JUST CLOSING IN AROUND?
A: NO, THE CAMPUS HERE IS VERY, VERY FREE

Q: DOES IT MAKE YOU ANGRY, THE WAY WAR IS DRAGGING ON?
A: WELL, I HOPE THE PRESIDENT KNOWS WHAT HE'S INTO, I DON'T KNOW

Q: DON'T YOU SEE STARVATION IN THE CITY WHERE YOU LIVE?
ALL THE NEEDLESS HUNGER? ALL THE NEEDLESS PAIN?
A: I HAVEN'T BEEN THERE LATELY, THE COUNTRY IS SO FINE
MY NEIGHBORS DON'T SEEM HUNGRY 'CAUSE THEY HAVEN'T GOT THE TIME

Q: THANK YOU FOR THE TALK MY FRIEND, YOU REALLY EASED MY MIND
I WAS WORRIED 'BOUT THE SHAPES OF THINGS TO COME
A: WELL IF YOU HAD MY OUTLOOK YOUR FEELINGS WOULD BE NUMB
YOU'D ALWAYS THINK THAT EVERYTHING WAS FINE
EVERYTHING IS FINE

ALL: WE CAN MAKE IT HAPPEN
WE CAN CHANGE THE WORLD NOW
WE CAN SAVE THE CHILDREN
WE CAN MAKE IT BETTER

GOODBYE

Studio City, California 1972

SELECTED LYRICS

FLYING HIGH
TOUCH THE SKY
GOING TO
PLACES I
NEVER KNEW
SO GOODBYE
AND "HELLO" LONG AGO

I CAN SEE
HISTORY
STANDING STILL
A MYSTERY
IF YOU WILL
PARDON ME
I'M AWAY FOR THE DAY

FEELS SO GOOD
TO BE SOARING
'CAUSE L.A. WAS SO BORING
GOODBYE
THERE MUST BE
ROOM FOR GROWING
SOMEWHERE ELSE AND I'M GOING
GOODBYE

THE DAYS AND THE NIGHTS
HAVE GONE DRY
THE LAST THREE WHOLE YEARS
HAVE FLASHED BY

SATURDAY IN THE PARK

Studio City, California 1972

SATURDAY IN THE PARK
YOU'D THINK IT WAS THE FOURTH OF JULY
PEOPLE DANCING, PEOPLE LAUGHING
A MAN SELLING ICE CREAM
SINGING ITALIAN SONGS
"EH CUMPARI, CI VO SUBARI"
CAN YOU DIG IT?
(YES I CAN)
AND I'VE BEEN WAITING SUCH A LONG TIME
FOR SATURDAY

ANOTHER DAY IN THE PARK
I THINK IT WAS THE FOURTH OF JULY
PEOPLE TALKING REALLY SMILING
A MAN PLAYING GUITAR
AND SINGING FOR US ALL
WILL YOU HELP HIM CHANGE THE WORLD
CAN YOU DIG IT?
(YES I CAN)
AND I'VE BEEN WAITING SUCH A LONG TIME
FOR TODAY

SLOW MOTION RIDERS FLY THE COLORS OF THE DAY
A BRONZE MAN STILL CAN TELL STORIES HIS OWN WAY
LISTEN CHILDREN, ALL IS NOT LOST
ALL IS NOT LOST, OH, NO

FUNNY DAYS IN THE PARK
EVERYDAY'S THE FOURTH OF JULY
PEOPLE REACHING, PEOPLE TOUCHING
A REAL CELEBRATION
WAITING FOR US ALL
IF WE WANT IT REALLY WANT IT
CAN YOU DIG IT?
(YES I CAN)
AND I'VE BEEN WAITING SUCH A LONG TIME
FOR THE DAY

ROBERT LAMM

SONG FOR RICHARD AND HIS FRIENDS

Studio City, California 1972

SELECTED LYRICS

IF YOU WILL THINK NOW, THEN YOU WILL SEE
HOW YOU CAN CHANGE THINGS
PEOPLE ARE WAITING, TURNING AWAY
TIRED OF KILLING

HEY NOW, WOULD YOU GO AWAY?
WE'RE SO TIRED OF THINGS THAT YOU SAY
EVEN THOUGH YOU NEVER SAID A WORD
THAT WOULD HELP ANYONE BUT YOURSELF
TOMORROW IS SUCH A BAD DREAM

IF YOU STAY NOW, THINGS WILL ONLY GET WORSE
LET US PRAY NOW
'CAUSE THE TRUTH REALLY HURTS
AFTER THE EVENTS OF TODAY WITH YOUR
BROTHERS AND YOUR SISTERS DEAD AND DYING
TOMORROW IS SUCH A BAD DREAM

PLEASE BE GONE
GO AWAY AND LEAVE US ALONE
BRAIN POLICE
GO AWAY AND LEAVE US IN PEACE

WHEN YOU GO NOW, WOULD YOU TAKE ALL YOUR FRIENDS
OH, NOW, IF YOU'D STOOD LIKE A MAN
EVEN THOUGH WE KNOW THAT YOU CANNOT BE BLAMED
ALL ALONE FOR THE SADNESS YOU'VE CAUSED
TOMORROW IS SUCH A BAD DREAM
YEAH, SUCH A BAD DREAM

SOMEDAY I'M GONNA GO

Hollywood, California 1973

SELECTED LYRICS

SOMEDAY I'M GONNA GO
SOMEDAY I'M GONNA GO
FARAWAY
FARAWAY
FARAWAY
FAR, FAR AWAY
I'M GONNA GO FARAWAY

DID YOU EVER WANT?
DID YOU EVER WANT TO RUN AND HIDE YOURSELF AWAY?
DID YOU EVER TRY?
DID YOU EVER TRY AND THERE WAS NOTHING
THERE WAS NOTHING
THERE WAS NOTHING THERE
NOTHING THERE

SOMEDAY I'M GONNA GO
SOMEDAY I'M GONNA GO
FARAWAY
FARAWAY
FARAWAY
FAR, FAR AWAY
I'M GONNA GO FARAWAY

ROBERT LAMM

HARRY TRUMAN

Caribou Ranch, Colorado 1975

AMERICA NEEDS YOU, HARRY TRUMAN
HARRY, COULD YOU PLEASE COME HOME?
THINGS ARE LOOKIN' BAD
I KNOW YOU WOULD BE MAD
TO SEE WHAT SORT OF MAN
PREVAILS UPON THE LAND YOU LOVE

AMERICA'S WONDERING HOW WE GOT HERE
HARRY, ALL WE GET IS LIES
WE'RE GETTIN' SAFER CARS
AND ROCKETSHIPS TO MARS
FROM MEN WHO'D SELL US OUT
TO GET THEMSELVES A PIECE OF POWER

WE'D LOVE TO HEAR YOU SPEAK YOUR MIND
IN PLAIN AND SIMPLE WAYS
CALL A SPADE A SPADE JUST LIKE YOU DID BACK IN THE DAYS
WHEN YOU WOULD PLAY PIANO
EACH MORNING WALK A MILE
SPEAK OF WHAT WAS GOIN' DOWN
WITH HONESTY AND STYLE

AMERICA'S CALLING, HARRY TRUMAN
HARRY, YOU'D KNOW WHAT TO DO
THE WORLD IS TURNING ROUND
AND LOSIN' LOTS OF GROUND
OH, HARRY IS THERE SOMETHING WE CAN DO
TO SAVE THE LAND WE LOVE?

SCRAPBOOK

Caribou Ranch, Colorado 1975

SELECTED LYRICS

SIX SETS SMOKED ON SATURDAYS
AT BARNABY'S ON STATE
COUNTLESS CALIFORNIA CALLS
WE COULD NOT STAND THE WAIT
WE PLAYED THE PIER ON VENICE BEACH
THE CROWD CALLED OUT FOR MORE
WITH ZAPPA AND THE MOTHERS NEXT
WE FINISHED WITH A ROAR

JIMI WAS SO KIND TO US
HAD US ON THE TOUR
WE GOT SOME EDUCATION
LIKE WE NEVER GOT BEFORE

AROUND THE WORLD IN TWENTY DAYS
WE PLAYED MOST EV'RY NIGHT
JET LAG, GIRLS, STRANGE LANGUAGES
EV'RYONE BEGAN TO FIGHT
LOWDOWN AT THE CARIBOU
ALL RUMORS ASIDE
WAS WE COULD NEVER GET TOGETHER
NOT UNLESS WE TRIED

SUMMER WITH THE BEACHBOYS
WE GOT SAND ALL IN OUR SHOES
WE MADE SOME SPECIAL MUSIC YEAH YEAH
EV'RYBODY SANG THE BLUES

TABLA

Coldwater Canyon, California 1988

SELECTED LYRICS

EARLY MORNING
THEY BROKE DOWN THE DOOR
OUT IN CHITTAGONG HILL
THE CITIZENS WERE POOR
RISING CONFLICT
IT WAS ELECTION TIME
OPPOSING BLOOD WAS SPILLED

PEOPLE OF CONSCIENCE
GATHERING IN PEACE
PRACTICED NON-VIOLENCE
PUT DOWN BY THE POLICE
SOME WERE LEADERS
MOST WERE SIMPLY THERE
OPPOSING VOICES STILLED
TABLA
AND WE ALL REMEMBER
TABLA
WHAT SHE DID FOR US
TABLA
SHE WAS THE BRAVEST ONE

SHE WAS A SIMPLE GIRL
BUT SHE WAS PUSHED TOO FAR
SHE WOULDN'T GIVE IN
AND THE TORTURE COULD NOT CHANGE HER MIND
AND WHEN THE PEOPLE HEARD
THEY ALL ROSE UP IN THE NAME OF LOVE
SINGING:
TABLA
AND WE ALL REMEMBER
TABLA
WHAT SHE DID FOR US
TABLA
SHE WAS THE BRAVEST ONE

WILL PEOPLE EVER CHANGE?

Greenwich Village, New York 1991

WOKE THIS MORNING, HAD IT MADE
MY SHEETS WERE CLEAN, MY RENT WAS PAID
OUT THE DOOR, WALKED DOWN THE STREET
PAVEMENT NEW BENEATH MY FEET
SET MY WATCH AHEAD A YEAR OR TWO
SET MY HEAD TO WATCHING WHAT THE WORLD WOULD DO

NEW PRESIDENT, BUT IT"S THE SAME
A DIFFERENT FACE, ANOTHER NAME
HALF OF FRIENDSHIP IS RECEIVE
IN GOD WE TRUST, IN BUCKS BELIEVE
WEIRD TO WATCH IT FROM THIS POINT OF VIEW
WEIRD FOR SURE, AND FUNNY, BUT IT SURE AIN'T NEW

SIGN ON THE STOREFRONT SAYS COME PUT YOURSELF IN DEBT
NOT TO WORRY, IN AMERICA YOU'RE FREE, JUST DON'T FORGET
PEOPLE PAY A PRICE FOR LIFE THAT OTHER PEOPLE SET
PEOPLE ARE SO STRANGE
BUT PEOPLE WILL BE PEOPLE
WILL PEOPLE EVER CHANGE?

THESE RANDOM MOMENTS OF CONTENT
WE HUNGER FOR, OUR SOUL IS SPENT
COME EACH DAY THEN DIE WITH SLEEP
THEIR MEMORY IN THE DARKNESS, WEEPS

ROBERT LAMM

IF EVERYBODY KNOWS

Greenwich Village, New York 1991

SELECTED LYRICS

A LITTLE SOMETHING JUST TO OPEN THE EYE
I HAD A 'TIME BUT IT SURE FLEW BY
CAUGHT A RIDE NOW I'M BACK IN TOWN AGAIN
GOT MY OLD JOB, IT FEELS LIKE HELL
MY LINE BUDDIES: THEY DON'T LOOK WELL
AND IT LOOKS LIKE PAIN

JOHNNY'S MARRIAGE IS ABOUT TO END
ALL INVOLVED WOULD RATHER JUST PRETEND
SING ALONG AND HAVE A DANCE OR TWO TONIGHT
IT'S NOT A DEAL LIKE ANYONE IS BROKEN
TIMES ARE FEW WHEN THE TRUTH GETS SPOKEN
SPOILING FOR A FIGHT

IF EVERYBODY KNOWS
YOU CAN'T GO HOME AGAIN
WHY DO I TRY?
I SHOULDA' LEARNED BY NOW
IT'S A DOOR THAT'S LOCKED
MY HANDS ARE RED FROM KNOCKIN'
IF EVERYBODY KNOWS
WHY DON'T I?

HEADING OUT TO WHERE THE FOUR WINDS PLAY
'CROSS THE DESERT AND THEY SEEM TO SAY
"SOMETIMES YOU GOT TO DO WHAT'S RIGHT"
HERE'S TO JOHNNY, HAVE A DRINK TO HIM
IN THE END HE'S GONNA SINK OR SWIM
GOD, SHINE DOWN YOUR LIGHT

GOT MY HEAD UP IN THE SKY: YOU COULD SAY I'M A DREAMER

THE LOVE OF MY LIFE

Greenwich Village, New York 1993

SELECTED LYRICS

SO MANY PEOPLE WITH A STORY TO TELL
THE WORLD'S FULL OF VICTIMS
AND IF YOU ASKED THEM WHAT THEY'RE TRYING TO SELL
THEY WANT TO DRAG YOU DOWN WITH THEM
THEY WANT TO DRAG YOU DOWN WITH THEM

IN THE END THE LOVE WE LIVE WITH
IS THE LOVE THAT WE WAIT FOR
AND THE WAITING CUTS LIKE A KNIFE
IN THE END THE LOVE WE HOPED FOR
IS THE LOVE THAT WE LEARNED WITH
LOOKING FOR THE LOVE OF MY LIFE
THE LOVE OF MY LIFE

THERE'S NOT A DAY WHEN I DON'T OPEN MY EYES
RANDOM MOMENTS OF FASHION
YOUR HEART WILL GUIDE ME WHEN MY HEAD TELLS ME LIES
I'VE STILL GOT THE PASSION
YOU KNOW I'VE STILL GOT THE PASSION

GOT TO TREASURE EVERY MOMENT
EVERY MOMENT IS A GOOD TIME
AND I NEVER HAVE NOTHING TO HIDE
GOT A SENSE OF SOMEONE WHO CARES
AUTOMATION IS DEADLY
LOOKING FOR THE LOVE OF MY LIFE
THE LOVE OF MY LIFE

NEVER MIND TOMORROW
IT'S ONLY A GYPSIES' FANTASY
TIME WE HAVE IS BORROWED
ONLY WANTING WHAT WE'RE NEEDING
NEEDING ONLY WHAT WE HAVE TODAY

SACHA

Greenwich Village, New York 1993

SELECTED LYRICS

YOU GOT YOUR BLUE EYES OPEN WIDE WITH WONDER
A WORLD YOU'VE NEVER SEEN BEFORE
THE LOVE, THESE FEELINGS AND THIS SPELL I'M UNDER
EACH DAY I LOVE YOU MORE AND MORE
SACHA MY LOVE
MY LITTTLE ONE
GENTLY I HOLD YOU TO MY HEART

I LOVE THE WAY YOU TRUST SO PURELY AND COMPLETELY
IT COMES SO NATURALLY TO YOU
YOU LOOK ME IN THE EYE AND SMILE SO SWEETLY
AS YOU DISCOVER SOMETHING NEW
SACHA MY LOVE
MY LITTLE ONE
GENTLY I HOLD YOU IN MY HEART

SACHA BABE, WE WAITED FOR YOU ALL THROUGH THE NIGHT
SACHA BABE, DON'T YOU KNOW IT WAS LOVE AT FIRST SIGHT
SACHA BABE, SINCE YOU'VE BEEN HERE I'M STARTING TO GET IT RIGHT

NOT MUCH TO SAY, JUST BIG BLUE EYES
SUCH ELOQUENCE DESPITE YOUR SIZE

YOU SEEM TO UNDERSTAND SO MUCH THAT I AM SAYING
WORDS CAN BE FRUSTRATING, I KNOW
SO WELL YOU SPEAK TO ME WHEN WE ARE PLAYING
SO SURE AND STEADILY YOU GROW
SACHA MY LOVE
MY LITTLE ONE
GENTLY I HOLD YOU TO MY HEART
BABY YOU, YOU, YOU

STANDING AT YOUR DOOR

Greenwich Village, New York 1993

SELECTED LYRICS

MOST OF MY LIFE
I WAS LIVING WITHOUT YOU
ON MY OWN
INDEPENDENT SON
NIGHTS I WOULD LIE AWAKE
I TRIED TO PICTURE THE MOMENT
I WOULD KNOW
WAS I THE ONLY ONE?
CONVERSATIONS OVERDUE
YEARS IN THE WAY

I STAND AT YOUR DOOR
I'M READY NOW
ALL OF THESE YEARS
JUST MARKING TIME
NOW I'M STANDING AT YOUR DOOR

I FELT LIKE A CHILD
AFRAID OF THE DARKNESS
NOW COMES THE LIGHT
AM I SUPPOSED TO CARE?
SOMETHING WENT WRONG
DID YOU COME TO FORGET ME?
CONVERSATIONS OVERDUE
YEARS IN THE WAY

I STAND AT YOUR DOOR
I'M READY NOW
ALL OF THESE YEARS
JUST MARKING TIME
WHAT ARE YOUR THOUGHTS?
WHAT DO YOU DO?
WHAT PART OF ME HAS COME FROM YOU?
NOW I'M STANDING AT YOUR DOOR

SLEEPING IN THE MIDDLE OF THE BED AGAIN

Greenwich Village, New York 1994

SELECTED LYRICS

CAUGHT IN A LOVESTORM
HOWL'N LIKE A NEWBORN
TRYIN' HARD TO STAY WARM
MY COVERUP IS TORN UP AND TATTERED
ADDICTION TO APOCALYPSE
LOOKING FOR THE BIG HIT
TENDING TO TAKE TRIPS
THE SHIP OF LOVE IS BEAT-UP AND BATTERED

TIME AFTER TIME
I BLOW ME AWAY
SIGNS ON THE STREET, NOW
BROTHER LET ME PRAY NOW
WINTER'S HERE
I BELIEVE IT'S HERE TO STAY

I READ SOMEWHERE THAT RELIGION IS FOR PEOPLE
WHO WANT TO STAY OUT OF HELL
I WAS PRAYING FOR A SIGN, OR A VISION, OR A MESSAGE
'TIL YOU BEEN THERE YOU WON'T GET WELL
I WAS SITTING IN A ROOM, I'D NEVER RECOGNIZE IT
WITH A PICTURE BEFORE MY EYES
I'VE BEEN SLEEPING IN THE MIDDLE OF THE BED AGAIN
I'M NOT SURE THIS QUALIFIES

LOST IN A CROSSWALK
BATTLE ONLY HALF-FOUGHT
CRAWLIN 'CAUSE I CAN'T TALK
CHILDHOOD FINALLY CAUGHT UP WITH ME
FLASHIN' LIKE A NEON
NOISY AS AN A-BOMB
LOOKING TO THE BEYOND
STARING INTO THE HALF-LIFE OF ETERNITY

FEEL THE SPIRIT

Greenwich Village, New York 1996

SELECTED LYRICS

I WAS ALL DRESSED UP
"ARE YOU SITTING DOWN?"
THE VOICE OF REASON ASKED
AND MY KNEES WERE SHAKING
AND MY HEART WAS BREAKING TOO

THEN THE NEWS CAME IN
HELP ME WITH MY SOUL
GO ON AND HURT A FRIEND
IT ONLY TOOK A MINUTE
BUT A LIGHTYEAR TO BEGIN IT

FROM MY EAR TO MY BRAIN IS A TORTUROUS ROUTE
I CAN'T SAY HOW MANY NIGHTS I CRY
FOR JUST A MOMENT, INCHES FROM THE LIGHT
AND YOUR DREAM SHOULD HAVE COME TRUE

CAN YOU FEEL THE SPIRIT?
THE DAWN BREAKS OVER THE WATER
CAN YOU FEEL THE SPIRIT?
NEW DAY IS COMING TO LIFE

OH MY GENTLE FRIEND
THE YEARS PASS SO FAST
ALL THE PAIN WAS SUCH A LOAD
THERE WAS NO JOY IN PLAYING
AND NO SENSE IN STAYING

NOW IT'S NOT DISTURBING THE PEACE WITH YOU
PLAYING FOR BLOOD, LIKE A MISSIONARY IN THE JUNGLE
AND I GUESS IT'S SOMETHING TO SURVIVE
NOW WE OPEN UP THE HEART MAKE IT BEAT AGAIN

CAN YOU FEEL THE SPIRIT?
THE DAWN BREAKS OVER THE WATER
FEEL THE SPIRIT
NEW DAY IS COMING TO LIFE

SAD OLD HOUSE

Greenwich Village, New York 1996

SELECTED LYRICS

THE SAD OLD HOUSE JUST DOWN THE ROAD
THERE, ON THE LEFT, I ALWAYS SEE IT
ALL THE AWNINGS FADED GRAY BY THE SUN

THE BRICK FACADE IS CRUMBLING
AND THE IRON FENCE NEEDS PAINT
THE YARD COULD USE SOME TENDING BY SOMEONE

A LITTLE RED TRICYCLE LAYS THERE
OVERTURNED AND VERY RUSTY
IT MAKES ONE WONDER WHERE ON EARTH THE RIDER HAS GONE

AND IN THE END
IT'S THE TIME WE ALWAYS SPEND
WONDERING WHERE THE HELL THE TIME GOES, ANYWAY?

A MAN NAMED YURGRAU SPUN MY HEAD
HE WROTE A STORY WHICH I READ:
HERE'S A MAN RETURNING HOME WITH A BOMB

A CLICHÉ TWIST WOULD SAVE HIM
QUITE A TIDY RESOLUTION
(THE BARD WILL CHOOSE AN ENDING AIMED TO STUN)

BUT, NO, IT BLEW HIM THROUGH THE ROOF
THE MAN, THE HOME, THE BOMB, ET CETRA
AND WHERE HE LANDED WAS THE START OF HIS LIFE!

AND IN THE END
IT'S THE TIME WE ALWAYS SPEND
WONDERING WHERE THE HELL THE TIME GOES, ANYWAY?

AND IN MY DREAM WHICH BEGAN LONG AGO
I TOLD MY HEART WHAT MY HEART COULD NOT KNOW
SO I CRIED WITH EVERY STEP AS I WALKED AWAY

I COULD TELL YOU SECRETS

Santa Monica, California 2001

SELECTED LYRICS

IF I SAY I LOVE YOU
NO ONE ELSE ABOVE YOU
IN A WORLD WITHOUT ROMANCE
HOW WOULD YOU KNOW?

ALL THINGS ARE CONNECTED
MUCH MORE THAN WE SUSPECTED
NOTHING IS BY CHANCE
HOW WOULD YOU KNOW?

I COULD BRING YOU FLOWERS
I COULD BRING YOU CANDY
I COULD TELL YOU STORIES
NO NO NO
I COULD WRITE YOU LETTERS
I COULD PAINT YOU PICTURES
I COULD TELL YOU SECRETS

SUBTLETY AND PASSION
HAVE FALLEN OUT OF FASHION
WITHOUT MORE THAN JUST A GLANCE
HOW WOULD YOU KNOW?
HOW WOULD YOU KNOW?

WE COULD TALK FOR HOURS
WE COULD EAT THAT CANDY
NO GUTS AND NO GLORY
OH!
I COULD WRITE YOU LETTERS
I COULD PAINT YOU PICTURES
I COULD TELL YOU SECRETS

I SEE NO CHANCE OF US BECOMING SOMETHING DULL
THIS EXTRAORDINARY FUNDAMENTAL WAY OF LOVE

IT'S A GROOVE, THIS LIFE

Greenwich Village, New York 2001

I'VE ALWAYS BEEN A DREAMER
I HIT THE FLOOR RUNNING
BUT I DON'T FORGET TO PRAY
JOY, SHE IS A COMER
SOON SHE'S GONNA HAPPEN
A THINKER WITH A LOT TO SAY
IT'S A GROOVE, THIS LIFE

MY DEAR FRIEND IS A DRINKER
TAN AND ALCOHOLIC
HIS BONES ARE BLEACHING IN THE SUN
MACKIE IS A SCHEMER
SAYS HE'S GOT SOME MUSIC
COULDN'T GET ARRESTED WITH A GUN
BUT IT'S A GROOVE, THIS LIFE
IT'S A GROOVE

IS IT RICH ENOUGH?
IS IT STRANGE ENOUGH?
IS IT FULL ENOUGH?
THIS LIFE
DO WE BITCH ENOUGH?
DO WE CHANGE ENOUGH?
IS IT FULL ENOUGH?
THIS LIFE

FRANKIE IS A DRIVER
PAST THE AGE OF REASON
USED TO BE A GREEN BERET
WHAT'S UP WITH THE SUMMER
BOOM! AND THEN IT'S OVER
GO AHEAD AND MAKE MY DAY
BUT IT'S A GROOVE, THIS LIFE
YEAH IT'S A GROOVE

I GET IMPATIENT WITH TOO MUCH TALK
LUCKY I CAN STILL WALK THE WALK
CAN'T BE RUNNING FROM THE DEVIL NOW
YOU TRY TO MAKE 'IM INTO YOUR FRIEND
FASTER AND FASTER YOU PLAY
CLOSE AND CLOSER YOU GET TO THE DAY
SO CLOSE TO THE END

FOR YOU, KATE

Santa Monica, California 2002

SELECTED LYRICS

I WAS LOST AND I WAS GOING NOWHERE
I WAS CAUGHT IN THE DRIFT OF CIRCUMSTANCE
I WAS CONSTANTLY WOND'RING, "WHAT'S IT ALL ABOUT, ALFIE?"
THEN I WAS GIVEN HALF A CHANCE

A LITTLE ANGEL CAME
I THINK I'D ALWAYS KNOWN HER NAME
I MUST HAVE DONE A REALLY REALLY GOOD THING
A NEVER REALLY UNDERSTOOD THING

I WAS READY FOR YOU KATE
I COULD HARDLY STAND THE WAIT
WHEN YOU FIRST CAME INTO VIEW
I SWEAR MY HEART KNEW WHAT TO DO
I WAS READY FOR YOU KATE
I'LL BE STEADY FOR YOU KATE
BIG GREEN EYES, A SEA OF BLUE
I'M SO AMAZED BY YOU

WHEN YOU SMILE YOU WARM THE COLDEST OF HEARTS
WHEN YOU SPEAK IT'S 'MISS ENCHANTMENT' ON THE PHONE
WHEN YOU TELL ME YOU MISS ME AS I'M TRAVELIN' THE ROAD
THEN IT'S SO GOOD TO GET BACK HOME

THE WISEST PEOPLE SAY
"YOU KNOW YOU MUST EMBRACE EACH DAY"
I CAN'T IMAGINE LIFE WITHOUT THIS FEELING
I NEVER, EVER, DOUBT THIS FEELING

YOU NEVER KNOW THE STORY

Santa Monica, California 2002

SELECTED LYRICS

I FIRST HEARD MILES PLAY
A MOST UNUSUAL WAY
I WATCHED, MY FRIEND AND I,
HIS UNCLE JUNKIE GET SO HIGH, SO HIGH

HE LEFT HIS RECORDS THERE
UNDER HIS FOLDING CHAIR
I TOOK THEM HOME WITH ME
I LISTENED AND THAT MUSIC STAYED WITH ME
YES, IT STAYED WITH ME.

YOU NEVER KNOW THE STORY
OF ANOTHER'S BROKEN HEART
WHAT WAS A SWEET ROMANCE
WAS SOMETHING 'MIGHT HAVE FELL APART
YOU NEVER KNOW THE COLOR
OF ANOTHER'S BROKEN DREAMS
THE ENDING OF A LOVE AFFAIR
MORE COSTLY THAN IT SEEMS

TERRY WAS A LUCKY MAN
A BIG HEART WITH A BIG PLAN
HIS LOVE PLAYED FAR AND WIDE
WHEN HE TURNED AWAY TO GO WE CRIED, WE CRIED

LIE TO OURSELVES TO LIVE
CHUMP REASONS THAT WE GIVE
TIME'S UP BEFORE YOU KNOW IT
GIVE UP THE GHOST AND LEARN IT'S LOVE
YES IT'S LOVE, IT'S LOVE

I THINK I FOUND A PART OF ME
A LITTLE PART OF ME, THAT I JUST LOST SOMEHOW
BRINGING UP SWEET MEMORIES OF OTHER DAYS
INTO MY HERE AND NOW

ANOTHER TRIPPY DAY

Greenwich Village, New York 2004

SELECTED LYRICS

THE CITY WAKES
A SLOW CRESCENDO
AND THE FLOOR BENEATH ME SHAKES
A DOWNTOWN TRAIN IS PASSING
AND IN MY DREAM
THE SUBWAY RUMBLE
DRIVES A CINEMATIC SCENE

OPEN MY EYES
A SILENT THUNDER
IN A ROOM I RECOGNIZE
A HINT OF DISTANT JAZZING
LOVERS EMBRACE
JUST BARELY MORNING
I TURN AND SEE HER FACE

THINK I'M HEADED FOR A TRIPPY DAY
GOT ME GROOVIN' AND I WANT TO SAY:
"COME ON COME ON
I WANT TO DANCE TONIGHT"

THINK I'M HEADED FOR A TRIPPY DAY
EVERYBODY GONNA FIND A WAY
COME ON COME ON
I WANT TO PLAY TONIGHT

OUT ON THE STREET
THE MUSIC GOOD THERE
AND YOU CAN'T DENY THE BEAT
THE DRUM LOOP GOT ME JUMPIN'
THE NEON GLOW
THE URBAN BUZZING
STILL, YOU ARE ALL I KNOW

LIFE IS FEELING LIKE SOME DREAMY FANTASY
AMBIENT AND INTIMATE, A PROPHESY
I NEVER KNEW SUCH SWEET TIMES
I MAY BE JUST A LUCKY FOOL

COME TO ME, DO

Manhattan, New York 2005 (For Sean)

SELECTED LYRICS

COME TO ME LONELY
COME TO ME BLUE
COME TO ME WEARY
COME TO ME, DO
I WILL REFRESH YOU
COME TO ME, DO
COME TO ME OFTEN
I'LL COME TO YOU
I'LL COME TO YOU

ALWAYS IN MY HEART
ALWAYS A SONG
THIS IS THE GOOD PART:
YOU'LL ALWAYS KNOW WHERE YOU BELONG
COME TO ME DARLIN
OOH BABY
COME TO ME DARLIN

COME TO ME HAPPY
COME TO ME BAD
COME TO ME LOOKING
FOR WHAT YOU'VE NOT HAD
I WILL SUSTAIN YOU
COME TO ME, DO
COME TO ME OFTEN
I'LL COME TO YOU
I'LL COME TO YOU

YOU ARE THE KIND ONE
I WAITED SO LONG
HOW DOES ONE FIND ONE?
YOU'LL ALWAYS KNOW WHERE YOU BELONG

ROBERT LAMM

I CONFESS

Manhattan, New York 2005

SELECTED LYRICS

I ALWAYS THINK OF VEGAS WHEN I POUR
MY COFFEE, JUST BEFORE
A SONG CALLED "JE T'ADORE"
PLAYS INSIDE MY HEAD

IT GIVES ME PEACE TO HEAR THE CRASHING SEA
MY DIGITAL SAYS '3'
I REALIZE I'M FREE
THIS IS PROBABLY GOOD

I CONFESS
I FEEL A SPIRIT STANDING BESIDE ME
I CONFESS
I JUST CAN'T SLEEP UNLESS I FEEL YOUR TOUCH
I CONFESS
A FULL MOON RISING, I MISS MY CHILDREN
I CONFESS
I CONFESS I LIVE A DREAMERS WAY

REDEYE RISES IN A COLD BLACK SKY
MY ANGELS STAY BEHIND
THE HEART, IT NEVER LIES
LONELINESS IS THE PROOF

I CONFESS
I SEE THE MAGIC IN EV'RY DAY NOW
I CONFESS
I HAVE BEEN GUILTY OF JUST LOOKIN' AWAY
I CONFESS
THE MIRACLE COMES OF HOW TO SAY THIS:
I CONFESS I LIVE A DREAMERS WAY

AND SO THE WORLD SEEMS QUIET TONIGHT
WHAT TOMORROW KNOWS WE WONDER
BUT THIS HEART IS GONNA BE ALRIGHT

HAUTE GIRL

Manhattan, New York 2006

SELECTED LYRICS

SO BRIGHT AND YOUNG
HAUTE GIRL SUSPECTS SHE'S BEAUTIFUL
HER EYES GIVE IT AWAY
YES THEY BETRAY HER INNOCENCE
LIVING IN THE DREAM
SHE WALKS ALONG THE AVENUE
THE AURA IS EXTREME
THE HUNGER EXTRAORDINARY

SO CLOSE TO FABULOUS
HAUTE GIRL HAS GOT AN ATTITUDE
A PRETTY COVER UP
OF LOVELY INSECURITY
IT GUARDS HER TENDER HEART
BUT STILL HER TENDER HEART CRIES OUT

PERHAPS, SHE LOST SOMEONE SHE LOVES
SOMEONE WHO HAD TO LEAVE
FOR JUST HIS OWN HEART'S SAKE
HIS LAST BEST CHANCE FOR LIFE
HIS LAST BEST CHOICE.
PERHAPS, HE WEPT AS HE WALKED AWAY
THERE IS A GOD IN HEAVEN
SHE KNOWS WILL BRING HER LOVE

AND SWEETNESS IN HER LIFE
HAUTE GIRL BELIEVES HER FANTASY
IN EVERY SENSE SHE HAS
HER WISHES ARE SPECTACULAR
WE FIND YOU FASCINATING
HAUTE GIRL

HEAVEN IN MY EYES

Manhattan, New York 2006 (Unfinished)

I, ACCUSTOMED TO THE WAIT
DRANK WHISKEY, ALWAYS LATE
BUT TIME WAS ON MY SIDE
LAUGHS WITH STRANGERS EVERY NIGHT
I BREATHED THE NEON LIGHT
SO MYSTIFIED

YOU WERE HEAVEN IN MY EYES
AND WHEN I SAW YOUR FACE
I KNEW THIS WAS MY LIFE

AND I, OBSESSED WITH SHALLOW DREAMS
RAN BRISKLY, SO IT SEEMS
STILL, YOU WERE KIND

YOU WERE HEAVEN IN MY EYES
AND WHEN I SAW YOUR FACE
I KNEW THIS WAS MY LIFE

YOU WERE HEAVEN IN MY ARMS
I FELT SUCH DEEP EMBRACE
I WAS LOOKING ALL MY LIFE

NOW I, WITH WHISPER AND A PRAYER
TO GODS, ADMIT TO CARE
COMPLETE AND OPEN EYED
WITH ALL THE DISMAY EVERYWHERE
I NEED YOU STANDING HERE
TO BRAVE THE NIGHT

SEAN, IT'S YOUR TURN

Manhattan, New York 2006 (Unfinished)

SELECTED LYRICS

DANCE, LITTLE GIRL
GONNA PLAY MY SAMBA
IT'S A MUSIC TO MAKE YOU MOVE
IT'S NOT A RAVE FOR YOUR KIND OF PARTY
BUT YOU KNOW HOW I LOVE THIS GROOVE

SMART AND STRONG
MY YOUNGEST ONE
HOW I ADORE YOUR FACE
DANCE FOR ME
FOR EVERYONE
YOUR SPIRIT IS YOUR GRACE

SEAN, IT'S YOUR TURN
HOW YOU MOVE WITH YOUR HEART TO THE SOUND
OH, SEAN, FIND YOUR LOVE
DANCE TO THE BEAT ALL AROUND

SWEETNESS WHEN WE
HAVE A LAUGH TOGETHER
I SURVIVE IN YOUR EYES SO BLUE
DEEP AND SO FIERCE I COULD FEEL YOUR COURAGE
NOW I WONDER WHAT YOU'RE GONNA DO

NOW AND THEN
I DRIFT AND DWELL
ON A SONG WE NEVER PLAYED
NEEDS UNSAID
YOU TURNED OUT WELL
I BOW TO CHOICES YOU MADE

SEAN, IT'S YOUR TURN
YOU WILL SEARCH FOR YOUR PLACE IN THE SUN
OH, SEAN, FIND YOUR LIFE
DANCE TO THE MUSIC

HALF A WORLD FROM ME NOW
MY HEART WAITS FOR YOU
MY ARMS ARE OPEN WIDE

THE POSSIBILITY OF LIFE

Manhattan, New York 2006

SELECTED LYRICS

THE POSSIBILITY OF LIFE
TO YESTERDAY: GOODBYE YOU KNOW
TODAY THIS IS A BRAND NEW SHOW
THE POSSIBILITY OF LIFE

RAINBOWS TO THE EAST
A SILKY SAMBA BEAT
DANCING EYES AND DANCING FEET
WE SEE A PURE MOON RISE
LIKE A MELODY
INSISTENT AND SO SWEET
THE QUESTION TO THE ANSWER IN YOUR EYES

SHIFTING TOWARDS THE MIST
THE SECRET OF A KISS
A CLOSING OF THE DISTANCE
IS THERE A SWEETER PRIZE?
THE CHILL AS WE BEGIN
DISCRETION SEEMS A SIN
ALL THE SCENES WE USED TO FANTASIZE

THERE'S EVERY POSSIBILITY
OF LIFE AND SO MUCH THERE TO SEE
AND WHEN YOU DON'T EXPECT IT TO
SOMETHING GOOD TAKES HOLD OF YOU
THE SUMMER SKY AT DUSK ALONE
A VOICE REMEMBERED ON THE PHONE
A CUP OF COFFEE WITH MY FRIEND
OH GOD I HOPE THIS NEVER ENDS

THE POSSIBILITY OF LIFE
A HOME, A HEART, A FAMILY
THIS IS THE WAY IT'S SUPPOSED TO BE
THE POSSIBILITY OF LIFE

SEND RAIN

Manhattan, New York 2010

SELECTED LYRICS

THE ROOM IS BLACK, AGAIN ALONE
MY HEART JUST CRIES
SEND RAIN, SEND RAIN
I GET SO TIRED, AGAIN I'M LOST
I ASK THE SKIES
SEND RAIN, SEND RAIN

HEADLINES SCREAM, THE TUBE JUST DRONES
I CLOSE MY EYES
SEND RAIN, SEND RAIN
EVERY CHOICE I EVER MADE
THE TRUTH DENIES
SEND RAIN, SEND RAIN

I PAY SO MUCH FOR RESTLESS SLEEP
THE ROOM SO HOT, THE TALK SO CHEAP
SO WASH AWAY AND QUENCH MY DOUBT
MY LIFE MY FAULT MY HUSH MY SHOUT

SUBTLE MOVEMENT BRINGS THE PAIN
THE GRAND DEMISE
SEND RAIN, SEND RAIN
AN ANGEL STANDS NOT FARAWAY
IT'S NO SURPRISE
SEND RAIN, SEND RAIN

4 BELLS

Austin, Texas 2011

SELECTED LYRICS

FOUR BELLS CHIME SOFT
IN A SILENT HOUSE
EMPTY, BUT FOR ONE BLUE BOY
JUST WAITING

FOUR BELLS CHIME SOFT
IT'S ALL BLUES TONIGHT
SOMETHING ENDS SOMETHING BEGINS
I'M WAITING

COLD EMPTY HEART
BUT I KNOW IT'S MY WORLD
TAKING THE TIME TO SAY GOODBYE

FOUR BELLS CHIME SOFT
NEVER YOUNG AGAIN
IN THE FURIOUS MOONLIGHT
I'M WAITING

COLD EMPTY HEART
BUT I KNOW IT'S MY WORLD
TAKING THE TIME TO SAY GOODBYE

GOODBYE, GOODBYE, GOODBYE, GOODBYE
THINK IT'S BETTER THAT I GO
GOODBYE, GOODBYE, GOODBYE, GOODBYE

GOODBYE, GOODBYE, GOODBYE, GOODBYE
DON'T KNOW WHEN I'LL SEE YOU AGAIN
GOODBYE, GOODBYE, GOODBYE, GOODBYE
SOMETHING LIKE I'VE GOT TO GO
GOODBYE, GOODBYE, GOODBYE, GOODBYE

OUT OF THE BLUE

Santa Monica, California 2011

SELECTED LYRICS

THERE'S A FIRE IN YOUR SOUL, BURNING
IT'S A PICTURE, IT'S A SONG
IN CREATING THERE IS LEARNING
WHAT YOU KNEW ALL ALONG

STILL A NOBLE QUESTION LINGERS
IS IT RIGHT? OR IS IT WRONG?
IN YOUR HEAD, YOUR HEART, YOUR FINGERS
THE PRESENCE OF YOUR ABSENCE IS SO STRONG

EVERYONE'S OBSESSED WITH TALKING EVERYWHERE
USELESS CONVERSATIONS IN THE AIR

OUT OF THE BLUE
I HEARD A WHISPER
I THOUGHT IT WAS YOU
I CAN'T BELIEVE HOW
IT'S YOU CALLING ME NOW
OUT OF THE BLUE

THERE'S A COSMIC MESSAGE BLINKING
TILT MY EAR AND TURN MY HEAD
I ALWAYS WONDER WHAT YOU'RE THINKING
I HEAR MUSIC INSTEAD

ALL WE ARE SEEING
AND ALL THAT WE KNOW
IS ALL ANCIENT DREAMING
FROM WHEN WE WERE HERE LONG AGO

OUT OF THE BLUE
I HEARD A WHISPER
I THOUGHT IT WAS YOU
I CAN'T BELIEVE HOW
IT'S YOU CALLING ME NOW
OUT OF THE BLUE

ONE DAY ON THE EQUINOX

Santa Monica, California 2011

SELECTED LYRICS

ONE DAY ON THE EQUINOX
I FOUND MYSELF STANDING ON THE EDGE
SUMMER WENT TOO FAST AND IT WAS TOO LATE

SO SWEET ON THE EQUINOX
ALWAYS WAS THAT WAY, TO ME
ALL THE LAZY NIGHTS OF SECRET PLEASURES

ONE NIGHT ON THE EQUINOX
YOU KNEW IT WAS TOO GOOD TO LAST
MAGIC JUST FOR US AND AIN'T WE LUCKY?

ONE DAY ON THE EQUINOX
ONE DAY ON THE EQUINOX

SPRING ARRIVES IN IT'S OWN SWEET TIME
WINTER ALWAYS WEARING OUT ITS WELCOME
RE-ENTRY INTO ATMOSPHERE MAY BRING SOME PAIN
AND THRILLS TO LAST A LIFETIME
ON THE EQUINOX

ONE DAY ON THE EQUINOX
IN EVERY QUARTER OF THE WORLD
DAY AND NIGHT TIME EQUAL DOWN TO THE MOMENT

THIS DAY ON THE EQUINOX
THE SUN APPEARS STILL IN THE SKY
SECRET JUST FOR US AND AIN'T WE LUCKY

ONE DAY ON THE EQUINOX
MAKING FRIENDS YOU'LL NEVER SEE AGAIN
GOOD PEOPLE, FACES, ALL IN THE MOMENT

ONE DAY ON THE EQUINOX
ONE DAY ON THE EQUINOX

WATCHING ALL THE COLORS IN MY HEAD

Santa Monica, California 2011

SELECTED LYRICS

HOW DO PEOPLE FIND THEIR LOVE?
LOVE AS IT WAS MEANT TO BE
WE WONDER IS IT FATE OR GODS ABOVE?
A CROWD OF PEOPLE STAND AND STARE
OBLIVIOUS WE COME TOGETHER

THE WHIPLASH OF THIS CITY STREET
A MILLION PEOPLE HAPPEN BY
GRAFFITI SWIRLING PRETTY, SWIRLING SWEET...
NOW, OUR WORLD IS NOT THE SAME
BUT I REMEMBER EVERY MOMENT
EVER, EVER

LONG AGO AND FARAWAY
EYES SO DEEP, WE KISS GOODNIGHT
THE SUBWAY TRAINS, "VIOLAU GAGO"
A CHRISTMAS MOON IN BLACK AND WHITE
STING OF TEARS, A SCARLET SKY
IT SEEMS I'M
WATCHING ALL THE COLORS IN MY HEAD

SITTING IN THE DARK WE SEE
IMAGES TO STUN, TO CRY
THE FURY OF THE SOUND, A SAMBA BEAT
HOW DO WE EMBRACE THE PAST?
I WILL REMEMBER EVERY MOMENT
EVER, EVER

NAKED IN THE GARDEN OF ALLAH

Santa Monica, California 2012

SELECTED LYRICS

WE ARE NAKED
WE ARE INNOCENT
WE ARE DEADLY
WE ARE BROKEN
WE ARE IGNORANT
WE ARE LOST

WE ARE CHILDREN
WE ARE DISCONTENT
WE ARE FATAL
WE ARE BROKEN
WE ARE IMPOTENT
WE ARE LOST

THIS TELEVISED DEMOCRACY
WE SEEK PROTECTION
SUCH ADOLESCENT FANTASY
WE SEEK REFUGE
RANDOM ACCESS TO CONTENT
I THINK WE'RE NAKED IN THE GARDEN OF ALLAH

WE ARE ARTLESS
WE ARE VIOLENT
WE ARE POISON
WE ARE BROKEN

PIE IN THE SKY AND GINGERBREAD
WE SEEK PROTECTION
WE NEVER MEANT TO GET IN BED
WE SEEK REFUGE
WITH WANNABE INTELLIGENCIA
I THINK WE'RE NAKED IN THE GARDEN OF ALLAH

JUST REMEMBER
I'LL REMEMBER

ABOUT THE AUTHOR

Robert was born and raised in Brooklyn, New York. As a child he heard the music of his parents' youth, jazz and Broadway musicals. At age 10, his mother enrolled him into the Grace Episcopal Boys' & Mens' Choir in Brooklyn Heights. In 1960 he relocated to Chicago, where he found jazz, rock, R&B and blues. While in high school, Robert formed a 4-piece band, singing and playing a Wurlitzer electric piano. Less than two years as a music-major at Roosevelt University in Chicago exposed him to classical works, and it was here that composing music became his primary interest.

It remains so to this day.

Robert was a founding member of Chicago, which began as an experiment in 1967. The band's debut album, "Chicago Transit Authority", was inducted into the Grammy® Hall of Fame (2014). Seven of the twelve songs on the album were his first compositions.

HONORS:

Elected to the American Society of Composers, Authors and Publishers 1971
Kennedy Center Founding Artist 1971
American Guild of Variety Artists 1974
Grammy Award 1974
American Music Award 1976
City of Chicago Medal of Merit 1976
American Music Award 1986
Hollywood Walk of Fame 1992
Key to the City of Chicago 1994
NARAS Governors Award 1996
Grammy Hall Of Fame 2014
Rock and Roll Hall of Fame 2016
Songwriters Hall of Fame 2017
Grammy Lifetime Achievement Award 2020

ROBERT LAMM

ACKNOWLEDGEMENTS

To all the dear people listed here, I owe a debt of gratitude… for their kindness, awesome professionalism and friendship. They were able to suspend disbelief in regard to my meager talents. All were willing to work magic resulting in my having a life, a family, a career, and rewards I had no right to expect, ever.

Bobby Woods / BMG Traci Butler / Mary Lee Ryan, Esq. / Peter Schivarelli / Irving Azoff / Tim Anderson / ASCAP / BMG Corey Brule / Gerry Beckley / Martin Brennan / Steve Brumbach / Dewey Bunnell / Bill Burns / Peter Cetera / Ned Colletti / Miss Millie Collins / Janet Schoen Crowley / Tom Cuddy / Neil Donell / Stan Eisenberg / Mike Engstrom / Bruce Fairbairn / Larry Fitzgerald / Jeffrey Foskett / David Foster / Mark Fried / Bill Gable / Bruce Gaitsch / Phil Galdston / Trent Gardner / Roland Gomez / Laurie Gorman / Jack Goudie / James William Guercio / Ray Herrmann / Billy Hinsche / Tatsu Hirano / Paul G. Hoffman, Esq. / Keith Howland / Hideyo Itoh / Tim Jessup / Zosia Karbowiak / Terry Kath / Lester Kaufman / Howard Kaufman / Nick Lane / Hank Linderman / Lee Loughnane / John McCurry / Anne Versteeg McKittrick / Gerard McMahon / Rick Mozenter / James Nederlander, Jr. / Amie O'Connor / Laudir deOliveira / James Pankow / Walter Parazaider / Lou Pardini / Dolores & Emil Pascarelli / Cheryl Pawelski / Phil Ramone / Walfredo Reyes, Jr. / Dennis Roach, Esq. / Brad Rosenberger / Jason Scheff / Suzie Smith / Jackson Sousa / Hank Steiger / Brett Steinberg, CAA / Ross Traut / John Titta / Koji Toyoda / Jim Vallance / Marcos Valle / John Van Eps / Guy Webster / Carl Wilson / Randall Wixen / Hawk Wolinski / Grace Church, Brooklyn Heights.

Another Rainy Day In New York City
Words and Music by Robert Lamm
© 1976 Lamminations Music (ASCAP)
All Rights Administered by BMG Rights Management (US) LLC.
Used by Permission. All Rights Reserved.

Another Trippy Day
Written by Robert Lamm and John Van Eps
© 2016 Blue Infinity Music (ASCAP), by arrangement with Wixen Music Publishing, Inc.
Used by Permission. All Rights Reserved.

Beginnings
Words And Music by Robert Lamm
© 1969 Lamminations Music (ASCAP)
All Rights Administered by BMG Rights Management (US) LLC.
Used by Permission. All Rights Reserved.

Come To Me, Do
Words and Music by Robert Lamm
© 2006 Primary Wave Lamm (ASCAP)
All Rights Administered by BMG Rights Management (US) LLC.
Used by Permission. All Rights Reserved.

Dialogue Pt. I + II
Words and Music by Robert Lamm
© 1972 Lamminations Music (ASCAP)
All Rights Administered by BMG Rights Management (US) LLC.
Used by Permission. All Rights Reserved.

Does Anybody Really Know What Time It Is?
Words and Music by Robert Lamm
© 1969 Lamminations Music (ASCAP)
All Rights Administered by BMG Rights Management (US) LLC.
Used by Permission. All Rights Reserved.

Fancy Colours
Words and Music by Robert Lamm
© 1970 Lamminations Music (ASCAP)
All Rights Administered by BMG Rights Management (US) LLC.
Used by Permission. All Rights Reserved.

Feel The Spirit
Words and Music by Robert Lamm, Peter Wolf, and Philip Galdston
© 2000 Primary Wave Lamm (ASCAP)
All Rights Administered by BMG Rights Management (US) LLC.
Used by Permission. All Rights Reserved.

For You, Kate
Words and Music by Robert Lamm
© 2002 Primary Wave Lamm (ASCAP)
All Rights Administered by BMG Rights Management (US) LLC.
Used by Permission. All Rights Reserved.

Goodbye
Words and Music by Robert Lamm
© 1972 Lamminations Music (ASCAP)
All Rights Administered by BMG Rights Management (US) LLC.
Used by Permission. All Rights Reserved.

Harry Truman
Words and Music by Robert Lamm
© 1975 Lamminations Music (ASCAP)
All Rights Administered by BMG Rights Management (US) LLC.
Used by Permission. All Rights Reserved.

Haute Girl
Words and Music by Robert Lamm and John Van Eps
© 2006 Primary Wave Lamm (ASCAP)
All Rights Administered by BMG Rights Management (US) LLC.
Used by Permission. All Rights Reserved.

I Confess
Written by Robert Lamm and Hank Linderman
© 2011 Blue Infinity Music (ASCAP), by arrangement with Wixen Music Publishing, Inc.
Used by Permission. All Rights Reserved.

I Could Tell You Secrets
Words and Music by Robert Lamm
© 2002 Primary Wave Lamm (ASCAP)
All Rights Administered by BMG Rights Management (US) LLC.
Used by Permission. All Rights Reserved.

If Everybody Knows
Words and Music by Robert Lamm and Philip Galdston
© 1992 Primary Wave Lamm (ASCAP)
All Rights Administered by BMG Rights Management (US) LLC.
Used by Permission. All Rights Reserved.

It's A Groove, This Life
Words and Music by Robert Lamm
© 2002 Primary Wave Lamm (ASCAP)
All Rights Administered by BMG Rights Management (US) LLC.
Used by Permission. All Rights Reserved.

The Love Of My Life
Words and Music by Robert Lamm and Jim Vallance
© 1999 Primary Wave Lamm (ASCAP)
All Rights Administered by BMG Rights Management (US) LLC.
Used by Permission. All Rights Reserved.

Naked in the Garden of Allah
Written by Robert Lamm and Hank Linderman
© 2016 Blue Infinity Music (ASCAP), by arrangement with Wixen Music Publishing, Inc.
Used by Permission. All Rights Reserved.

On the Equinox
Written by Robert Lamm
© 2011 Blue Infinity Music (ASCAP), by arrangement with Wixen Music Publishing, Inc.
Used by Permission. All Rights Reserved.

Out of the Blue
Written by Robert Lamm and Trent Gardner
© 2011 Blue Infinity Music (ASCAP), by arrangement with Wixen Music Publishing, Inc.
Used by Permission. All Rights Reserved.

SELECTED LYRICS

The Possibility of Life
Written by Robert Lamm
© 2006 Blue Infinity Music (ASCAP), by arrangement with Wixen Music Publishing, Inc.
Used by Permission. All Rights Reserved.

Questions 67 and 68
Words and Music by Robert Lamm
© 1969 Lamminations Music (ASCAP)
All Rights Administered by BMG Rights Management (US) LLC.
Used by Permission. All Rights Reserved.

Sacha
Words and Music by Robert Lamm
© 1999 Primary Wave Lamm (ASCAP)
All Rights Administered by BMG Rights Management (US) LLC.
Used by Permission. All Rights Reserved.

Sad Old House
Words and Music by Robert Lamm and William Champlin
© 2002 Primary Wave Lamm (ASCAP)
All Rights Administered by BMG Rights Management (US) LLC.
Used by Permission. All Rights Reserved.

Saturday In The Park
Words and Music by Robert Lamm
© 1972 Lamminations Music (ASCAP)
All Rights Administered by BMG Rights Management (US) LLC.
Used by Permission. All Rights Reserved.

Scrapbook
Words and Music by Robert Lamm
© 1976 Lamminations Music (ASCAP)
All Rights Administered by BMG Rights Management (US) LLC.
Used by Permission. All Rights Reserved.

Sean
Words and Music by Robert Lamm
© 2006 Primary Wave Lamm (ASCAP)
All Rights Administered by BMG Rights Management (US) LLC.
Used by Permission. All Rights Reserved.

Send Rain
Words and Music by Robert Lamm
© 2007 Primary Wave Lamm (ASCAP)
All Rights Administered by BMG Rights Management (US) LLC.
Used by Permission. All Rights Reserved.

Sleeping In The Middle Of The Bed
Words and Music by Robert Lamm, John McCurry, and Oyewole
© 1994 Primary Wave Lamm (ASCAP)
All Rights Administered by BMG Rights Management (US) LLC.
Used by Permission. All Rights Reserved.

Someday I'm Gonna Go
Words and Music by Robert Lamm
© 1973 Lamminations Music (ASCAP)
All Rights Administered by BMG Rights Management (US) LLC.
Used by Permission. All Rights Reserved.

A Song For Richard And His Friends
Words and Music by Robert Lamm
© 1972 Lamminations Music (ASCAP)
All Rights Administered by BMG Rights Management (US) LLC.
Used by Permission. All Rights Reserved.

Standing At Your Door
Words and Music by Robert Lamm and John Van Eps
© 1993 Primary Wave Lamm (ASCAP)
All Rights Administered by BMG Rights Management (US) LLC.
Used by Permission. All Rights Reserved.

Tabla
Words and Music by Robert Lamm and Randy Goodrum
© 1988 Primary Wave Lamm (ASCAP)
All Rights Administered by BMG Rights Management (US) LLC.
Used by Permission. All Rights Reserved.

Watching All the Colors
Written by Robert Lamm and Lou Pardini
© 2016 Blue Infinity Music (ASCAP), by arrangement with Wixen Music Publishing, Inc.
Used by Permission. All Rights Reserved.

Will People Ever Change?
Words and Music by Robert Lamm
© 1993 Primary Wave Lamm (ASCAP)
All Rights Administered by BMG Rights Management (US) LLC.
Used by Permission. All Rights Reserved.

You Never Know The Story
Words and Music by Robert Lamm and Marty Grebb
© 2003 Primary Wave Lamm (ASCAP)
All Rights Administered by BMG Rights Management (US) LLC.
Used by Permission. All Rights Reserved.

4 Bells
Written by Robert Lamm
© 2011 Blue Infinity Music (ASCAP), by arrangement with Wixen Music Publishing, Inc.
Used by Permission. All Rights Reserved.

25 Or 6 To 4
Words and Music by Robert Lamm
© 1970 Lamminations Music (ASCAP)
All Rights Administered by BMG Rights Management (US) LLC.
Used by Permission. All Rights Reserved.

Marmont Lane Books would like to thank Tom Andre,
Andrew Golomb, and Cynthia Bell
for their assistance in the making of this book.

MARMONTLANE.COM

www.ingramcontent.com/pod-product-compliance
Lightning Source LLC
Chambersburg PA
CBHW081324040426
42453CB00013B/2299